S0-EGS-154

BLUEBACK

BY
COMMANDER SCOTT C. S. STONE
(USNR·RET)
COVER ART BY FORMER NAVYMAN ARTHUR E. (GENE) ELLIS

COPYRIGHT © 2000 BY SCOTT C.S. STONE

ALL RIGHTS RESERVED, INCLUDING THE RIGHT TO REPRODUCE THIS WORK IN ANY FORM WHATSOEVER
WITHOUT PERMISSION IN WRITING FROM THE PUBLISHER, EXCEPT FOR BRIEF PASSAGES
IN CONNECTION WITH A REVIEW.

FOR INFORMATION, WRITE:
The Donning Company/Publishers
184 Business Park Drive, Suite 106
Virginia Beach, VA 23462

STEVE MULL, *General Manager*
BARBARA A. BOLTON, *Project Director*
PAM FORRESTER, *Project Research Coordinator*
DAWN V. KOFROTH, *Assistant General Manager*
SALLY DAVIS, *Editor*
RICK VIGENSKI, *Graphic Designer*

LIBRARY OF CONGRESS CATALOGING · IN · PUBLICATION DATA:

AVAILABLE UPON REQUEST.

PRINTED IN THE UNITED STATES OF AMERICA

A gallant warrior at rest, the submarine lies at her dock by the Oregon Museum of Science and Industry on the banks of the Willamette River in Portland, Oregon, a long way from the exotic seas she has cruised beneath, and years away from her launching date. Now in an important but more sedate role, the USS Blueback (SS-581) has earned her repose; her hull pushed through waters that were unfriendly, her periscope has looked upon enemy ships and hostile coasts. Some of her work remains secret in the annals of the Navy, and all of it contributed to maintaining the freedom of the seas.

She was the last of her kind, the last submarine built before technology mandated the new breed of nuclear subs. Still, she represented a progression; the Blueback was one of the first subs to be built with the tear drop hull design, allowing for more speed and maneuverability.

To show her abilities, the submarine set a record by cruising entirely submerged from Yokosuka, Japan, to San Diego, a distance of 5,340 miles.

In her heyday the submarine took part in civic activities, proudly representing the Navy in fetes and observances, as willing a participant in peacetime missions as she was a strong force for America in the chilling days of the Cold War. Now she continues to serve her country, as a reminder of the never-ending need for vigilance and the continued requirement for sea power to keep a nation free.

The year 1959, a twisting, dangerous time: Fidel Castro became Cuba's dictator and embarked on a relationship with the Soviet Union that put America in hazard. The Dalai Lama was forced to escape to India and the Chinese puppet government in Tibet sealed the border. The Communist Party made dramatic gains in Indonesia, and Moscow urged Japan to forbid U.S. bases on Japanese soil and to accept Soviet "permanent neutrality." On May 16 of that turbulent year a new submarine with a tear-drop-shaped hull was launched and commissioned on October 15. She had been built by Ingalls Shipbuilding Corporation of Pascagoula, Mississippi, her keel laid on April 15, 1957, and sponsored by Mrs. Kenmore McManes, the wife of a Rear Admiral. The sub was headed for duty with the Pacific Submarine Force, the powerful, silent undersea component of the U.S. Pacific Fleet, and would be home-ported at Pearl Harbor in the Hawaiian Islands. Coincidentally in the same year, 1959, Hawaii became the fiftieth State.

The submarine was the USS *Blueback* (SS–581) a Barbel class diesel/electric sub, the last class of diesel submarines built by the U.S. Navy, which afterwards embarked on an ambitious program of building nuclear submarines. Nevertheless, the *Blueback* was anything but obsolete at the time of her launching. Her innovative hull shape gave her speed and maneuverability under the surface of the sea, and she carried six twenty-one-inch torpedo tubes and eighteen torpedoes. The tubes were kept loaded at all times. She had two General Electric Motors and a diesel fuel capacity of 112,000 gallons, and she later proved her abilities in a record-shattering 5,340-mile run from Yokosuka, Japan, to San Diego, California—all underwater.

The *Blueback* was the second U.S. Navy submarine to bear that name. The first was a Balao class sub designated (SS–326) commissioned in 1944. She was longer than the later *Blueback*, but lacked the more sophisticated sonar and ancillary equipment. The *Blueback* that joined the Pacific Fleet and was poised for her first deployment, was the most able and powerful submarine of her time. She sailed in harm's way under her first commanding officer, Lieutenant Commander R. H. Gautier.

In March 1961, the *Blueback* left her home port and pushed west through the Pacific, the world's mightiest ocean covering more than half the world's surface. She began to operate with the U.S. Seventh Fleet in a year that saw increasing East-West tensions; the Berlin Wall was built in August of that year, the Bay of Pigs disaster embarrassed the United States and heightened the already tentative relations with both Cuba and the Soviets, and out in the Soviet area of Novaya Zemlya, the Russians tested a massive thermonuclear device. The sub was a welcome asset in a time and place in which constant vigilance was mandatory, and the *Blueback* slipped stealthily through Asian waters, the silent eyes and ears of the Fleet.

For six months the *Blueback* prowled and probed. Mission completed, the submarine turned homeward, and her epic undersea voyage back to America illuminated both the capabilities of the sub and the awesome distances of the far Pacific. It was an auspicious beginning.

In April 1963, the *Blueback* again deployed to WESTPAC—the Navy's acronym for Western Pacific—and took part in the Coral Sea Festival, which included a visit to Australia, where she received an enthusiastic welcome. Again in 1967 and 1968 the submarine was a forward line of defense in WESTPAC, completing two full deployments.

Beginning in 1964 a nervous twenty-two-year-old Ensign spent eighteen months on the sub, learning how to be a submariner. Thirty years later John H. Dalton revisited the *Blueback* as Secretary of the Navy. "Serving on the *Blueback* was an exciting time for me," Dalton recalled to a reporter. "We had a great crew and it's a great ship. My time aboard was a very positive experience for me." Dalton went on to serve on a nuclear sub before leaving the Navy to pursue a business career, but he never forgot the relationships aboard the *Blueback* and the recognition and awards won by the sub during operations.

Being operational in distant seas could mean any number of things, such as conducting maneuvers with other U.S. submarines or surface ships. Or monitoring the movement of enemy vessels, perhaps photographing new enemy assets, testing new equipment and/or tactics, conducting joint operations with friendly navies, and operations classified then and now. *Blueback* was equal to the various tasks. Through the sub's periscope appeared the harbors of Murmansk and Vladivostok, sites in the Caribbean and the South Pacific, and enemy ships during the height of the Cold War.

In 1970 and 1971 the *Blueback* was again in Eastern seas, beginning now to accumulate awards attesting to her efficiency. A prestigious award was the Meritorious Unit Commendation, added to two consecutive Battle Efficiency "E" awards. In the next deployment in 1973, her seventh tour of duty in WESTPAC, she picked up her fourth consecutive Fire Control Excellence Award.

The year 1977 was a significant one for the *Blueback*. It was the year her home port was changed from Pearl Harbor to San Diego, and in July the sub left on a four-month deployment in which she sailed more than 13,000 miles, twice transiting the Panama Canal. In a well-planned operation she conducted anti-submarine exercises with the navies of Colombia, Ecuador, Peru, and Chile. The following year this versatile submarine was in Portland, Oregon, representing the Submarine Force at the Rose Festival with no one anticipating she was in what would be her final home.

The *Blueback*'s eighth and ninth WESTPAC deployments followed, the latter duty in which she was awarded a Supply "E" and Submarine Group Five's Top Gunner Award. The latter deployment came in 1980, the beginning of what many military men were calling "the dangerous decade" for all the potential hot-spots around the world.

The first year of the decade seemed to bear them out. A U.S. attempt to rescue fifty-three hostages held in Teheran ended in disaster when six C-130 aircraft from a base in southern Egypt landed ninety commandoes in the desert three hundred miles southeast of Teheran. A sandstorm and mechanical problems knocked out three of the operation's eight helicopters. Eight men were killed when a helicopter and a C-130 collided on the ground. The Ayatollah Khomeini threatened to kill the hostages if America tried again.

The Shah of Iran died of cancer, removing a man who had been a friend of the U.S. Iraq and Iran began a war that would last eight years. Polish shipyard workers at Gdansk went on a strike that spread to some 350,000 workers, and the Solidarity movement became the first independent labor union in a Soviet bloc country, but the Soviet Union massed fifty-five divisions on Poland's borders and the situation remained tense.

The *Blueback* maintained her posture of vigilance, but found time to return to Portland for the Rose Festival in 1981, representing the Submarine Force and drawing a sizeable number of visitors. Later that same year she was awarded the Fleet Communications "C" in recognition of superior performance in communications.

For the tenth and last time the *Blueback* turned her bow toward WESTPAC. It was January 1982, and one of the most interesting of her voyages. The sub sailed some 20,000 miles in carrying out operations with surface units of the U.S., Japanese, and Korean navies. It seemed the more the submarine sailed, the more awards she garnered, for in 1984 the *Blueback* won the Damage Control "DC" and the Supply "F" honors from Commander, Submarine Force Pacific. The next year the sub was awarded the Engineering Efficiency "E" and Communications "C" awards. She ended that year by operating with other Navy units and visited Vancouver, Canada, and Pearl Harbor and Lahaina, Maui, in the Hawaiian Islands.

A memorable year was 1988, in which the *Blueback* kept operating at full capacity—and winning more honors. In addition to the second consecutive Engineering Efficiency "E" the sub received an Anti-submarine Warfare "X" and the coveted Golden Anchor award from the Commander-in-Chief, U.S. Pacific Fleet. In that same year the *Blueback* paid port calls to Avalon on Santa Catalina Island off the California coast, to San Francisco, Seattle (twice), Monterey, and to Vancouver in Canada's British Columbia.

The following year the sub made her first port call to Juneau, Alaska, the first submarine to visit there in some thirty years, and meanwhile, her extraordinary performance kept earning her honors—another "E" award, another "C", a Supply "E" and the Pacific Fleet's Silver Anchor Award.

By now the *Blueback* was an aging vessel, still swift and powerful but approaching the time to retire. She had sailed countless miles, won a plethora of awards, and served her country well in far seas. She had operated with foreign navies, helped refine anti-submarine warfare—no small contribution in the face of a powerful Soviet submarine threat—and been a significant deterrent during the dangerous years of the Cold War.

CONTINUED ON PAGE 13

FROM UNDERSEA TO SURFACE
(HOW A SUBMARINE WORKS)

Even in the days of spacecraft and satellites, submarines continue to be among the most amazing (and mysterious) large-sized machines. They are at home on the surface of the sea, yet most comfortable deep in the dark of the ocean, propelled by nuclear energy, seeing by way of electronic devices.

The *Blueback* as one of the Barbel-class submarines, was given a Tear Drop design hull, an innovative hull design that permitted greater speed and maneuverability. With these advantages the submarine was a strong asset in the U.S. arsenal. For all her advanced technology, the *Blueback*—like all other submarines—operated on the same principals as John Holland's undersea craft back in 1895 and 1900: to submerge you take on ballast, to surface you get rid of it. (Ballast is the weight you use to make the submarine heavier than the water it displaces, so that it sinks beneath the surface.) When the *Blueback* was on the surface the ballast tanks were full of air (the sub had six tanks) keeping the sub afloat by positive buoyancy. When the sub was to be submerged, vents in the tanks were opened and the tanks filled with seawater making the submarine heavier than the water it displaced. The sub headed downward. Diving planes located on the sail and stem were angled downward, making the sub dive faster. At the desired depth, the crew could control the submarine by the sail and stem planes and trim system. This was negative buoyancy—adding ballast in the form of seawater so the submarine would submerge.

To achieve neutral buoyancy—that delicate balance between positive and negative—meant the submarine could stay below the surface without going deep, and travel about underwater without moving up or down. In this condition the submarine can be controlled, i.e., made to go up or down, by use of the diving fins.

To surface, compressed air was blown into the ballast tanks, forcing the water out, bringing the submarine again into a condition of positive buoyancy. Now the diving planes were angled upward, for speedier surfacing. The *Blueback* and other subs had entire banks of high-pressure air tanks to operate the pneumatic systems. In an emergency, air could be released directly into the ballast tanks located in various places of the submarine, bringing the submarine to the surface faster.

*The Blueback at christening begins her move toward her natural element,
the sea, at her launching on May 16, 1959.*
Photo courtesy Ingalls Shipbuilding Corporation.

The Blueback *was built by Ingalls Shipbuilding Corporation of Pascagoula, Mississippi, and christened by her sponsor, Mrs. Kenmore McManes, wife of a Rear Admiral.* U.S. Navy photo.

Birth of a submarine: the Blueback slides into the water immediately after christening. Photo courtesy of Ingalls Shipbuilding Corporation.

The submarine's sponsor, Mrs. Kenmore McManes, receives a bouquet from the Blueback's first commanding officer, Lieutenant Commander R. H. Gautier. U.S. Navy photo.

The commissioning crew assembles aboard the Blueback prior to what submarines call the "angles and dangles" cruise—the sub's shakedown cruise.
Photo courtesy Ingalls Shipbuilding Corporation.

In October 1990, the *Blueback* was decommissioned and berthed at Puget Sound Naval Shipyard in Bremerton, Washington. She did have another moment of glory: she was seen in the 1990 film, *The Hunt for Red October*, portraying the U.S. submarine *Dallas*. The film was another in a series of more than a dozen films in which submarines played a vital role. The *Blueback* was used in the film, one official explained, because it was the only ship left in the Fleet that had six torpedo tubes forward. "All the new subs," he said, "the torpedoes go off to the side. The interior scenes in the movie that show torpedo tubes had to use the *Blueback* as a setting."

For three years officials of the Oregon Museum of Science and Industry worked with Navy officials, and in February 1994, received formal possession of the submarine. She was towed from Bremerton to Portland, to become a vital part of OMSI's science education mission. The rationale was simple—as much knowledge as science had gained, there was still a lot to be learned about the planet's oceans. Submarines such as the *Blueback* were an important aspect of developing advanced sonar, life-support, mechanical and electronic systems required for undersea exploration, and such developments helped unlock the ocean's mysteries.

OMSI wanted the public to be able to go aboard a submarine and explore the complex machinery and technology. A spreading knowledge could only be beneficial in understanding the oceans and civilization's impact on them. Submarine veterans and U.S. Senator Mark Hatfield (R-Ore) helped OMSI acquire the *Blueback*, and OMSI spent more than a million dollars, for construction of a public access dock. Parts of the submarine were stripped of all equipment having to do with communications, cryptography and Intelligence-gathering, but a minimum of modifications were made before the *Blueback* was put on display, for OMSI wanted to keep the sub as authentic as possible.

No one who served aboard the *Blueback* will forget her, or the relationships formed by men involved in a difficult, dangerous and ultimately rewarding profession. There was the unusual environment, hundreds of feet beneath the sea, contained by the pressure hulls and knowing that a bad decision or a false move or even a simple mistake could put the submarine in hazard. There was the confined space—men having to "hot bunk" i.e., off watch sleeping in a bunk vacated by a man going on watch because the submarine couldn't provide enough bunk space. There was the necessity for cross-training and refresher training, the need to qualify in a technologically-advanced vessel, the close quarters.

And there was the mission. The *Blueback* might be at sea for anywhere from a week to two-and-a-half months. Some of that time would be focusing on an unfriendly shore.

On her very first sea-trials, the Blueback performs up to Navy expectations.
Photo courtesy Ingalls Shipbuilding Corporation.

THE 'BARBEL' CLASS

Submariners affectionately called them "The B Girls"— the diesel/electric submarines USS *Barbel* (SS-580), the USS *Blueback* (SS-581), and the USS *Bonefish* (SS-582). With their innovative Tear Drop hull design they had heightened maneuverability, and carried the latest communications, sonar, and cryptography equipment. The last class of diesel boats built before the Navy began constructing nuclear subs, the "B Girls" were considered the finest subs of their dangerous era.

The *Barbel* was launched July 19, 1958, and commissioned on January 17, 1959, sponsored by Mrs. Bernard L. Austin. She carried eight officers and sixty-nine enlisted men under the command of Lieutenant Commander Ord Kimzey, Jr. She was decommissioned on December 4, 1989, after more than thirty years of service and struck from the Navy list on March 4,1992.

The *Bonefish* was launched on November 22,1957, sponsored by Mrs. Lawrence L. Edge. Commissioned on July 9,1959, carrying eight officers and 69 enlisted men under the command of Lieutenant Commander Elmer H. Kiehl, she served nearly thirty years with the Fleet. The *Bonefish* was decommissioned on September 28,1988, as a result of a fire on board. The fire took the lives of three crewmembers while eighty-nine others were rescued. The sub was towed to Charleston, South Carolina, where it was determined her damages were too extensive to warrant repair, and decommissioning followed. She was the second sub to bear that name; Bonefish is the name of a sturgeon. Submarines were named for fish until the 1970s.

The *Blueback* is named for a salmon. As noted elsewhere, she was launched on May 16, 1959, commissioned October 15, 1959, and served for more than thirty years. She was decommissioned on October 1, 1990, and assumed her new role as a floating museum and memorial.

Recalled retired Chief Electronics Technician James R. (Pat) Patterson, who served aboard the *Blueback* from November 1977 to June 1981: "What we would do, we would go up there off the coast of Siberia and we would stick our ECM (electronic counter-measures) mast out and we'd pick up all these different kinds of radar and stuff. By going up and down the coast constantly, and picking up and classifying these different kinds of radar, we could tell basically where these radars were stationed. We would try to come in as close to the coast as we thought we could."

The sub would be traveling submerged. In time, Patterson remembered, the long surveillance runs up and down the Siberian coast were turned over to the new nuclear submarines. Other duties involved tracking, and Patterson recalled the effects of water temperature in submarine operations: "Sound travels through water at different speeds depending on the temperature of the water. So when you go from one temperature to another, it's going to change the speed of the sound. And you can actually get it to bounce. Sometimes you can hear a contact—we've heard surface contacts—for hundreds of miles, and track them because the sound travels as though it were in a tunnel." It was a cat-and-mouse game with enemy shipping, part of the whole sphere of Intelligence-gathering so vital to successful defense. Sometimes, the *Blueback* would have Intelligence officers on board, but whether Navy officers or civilians in Navy uniforms, the crew never knew. Patterson loved his sea duty. "I wouldn't have traded it for anything else in the world," he said. He noted that submariners needed a sense of humor because of the confinement and long tours at sea, and he approved of the rivalry between submariners and surface sailors: "There's always been competition between the skimmers and the subbers. It's what makes both of us better."

Richard N. (Dick) Hansen remembers operations that include looking at the potential enemy up close and personal. "When I went aboard we pulled a surveillance op in the Yellow Sea off the mouth of the Yangtze River . . . electronic and visual surveillance." Hansen was the engineering officer aboard the *Blueback* from 1967 through 1969, and before that was an enlisted man, a sonarman. He had duty on other ships and submarines, but remembers the *Blueback* as the best of them all.

"I don't know how to explain it," he told an interviewer, "other than to say it was the best submarine we ever served aboard. We had the best crew, the most closely cohesive group of people. It was family, there's no other way to explain it . . . when we had the dedication of the *Blueback* we had a reunion in Portland of the B-girls (the *Blueback*, *Barbel* and *Bonefish* crews) and who showed up most? Sailors from the *Blueback*."

Hansen also recalls fondly the capabilities of the *Blueback*. "We had more maneuverability than the old boats. The big advantage to the *Blueback* hull was that it was hydrodynamically designed so that you run submerged. We had a snorkeling capability in which you could run three engines full speed—made possible by the larger snorkel air intake . . . the design of the ship was such that it was probably better to run at snorkeling depth than on the surface. In fact, you could get greater speed submerged than you could on the surface. You could run faster fully submerged but only for a short time because you're running on batteries then." (Snorkeling is running just below the surface with the snorkel and other necessary masts extended from the water.)

Fully submerged the submarine could run at twenty-one or twenty-two knots (about twenty-five miles per hour) Hansen said.

CONTINUED ON PAGE 25

The Blueback wears a traditional lei of flowers around her sail after arrival home to Pearl Harbor after a deployment in the western Pacific.
U.S. Navy photo.

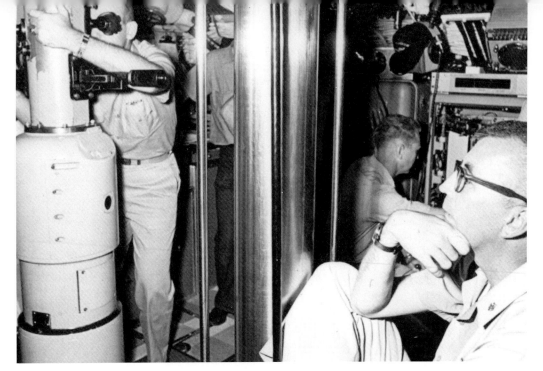

In close quarters and underway, ship's company maintains a periscope watch. U.S. Navy photo.

A Blueback crewman monitors a bewildering variety of gauges and switches; submarine training makes the crewman at home with a wide variety of controls. U.S. Navy photo.

A Lieutenant scans a control panel as the submarine cruises underwater. Note the ever-present coffee cup. U.S. Navy photo.

A Petty Officer mans the diving ballast controls while the Blueback is underway. Ballast, in the form of seawater, aids the submarine's diving capacity. U.S. Navy photo.

The COBs, Chief of Boat—relax and swap sea stories; these men are the last COBs of the diesel submarines; the new COBs reported to nuclear boats.
U.S. Navy photo.

The third of the "B girls," the USS Bonefish prowls the oceans. With the Blueback and Barbel, they represented the last of the diesel submarines before the Navy went to an all nuclear submarine fleet. U.S. Navy photo.

Relaxation comes later, while underway the sub's crew keeps a sharp eye on the submarine's instruments in the control room. U.S. Navy photo.

The end of an era: The Blueback is decommissioned in San Diego. U.S. Navy photo.

In drydock, the sub is given a coating of primer before the final coats are applied. Photo courtesy of R. G. Walker.

The Blueback's main hull gets needed repairs from a welder during the sub's drydock period in 1998. Photo courtesy of R. G. Walker.

A crew from the Oregon Museum of Science and Industry loads a display-model Mark 14 torpedo into the forward torpedo loading hatch for public viewing. Photo courtesy of R. G. Walker.

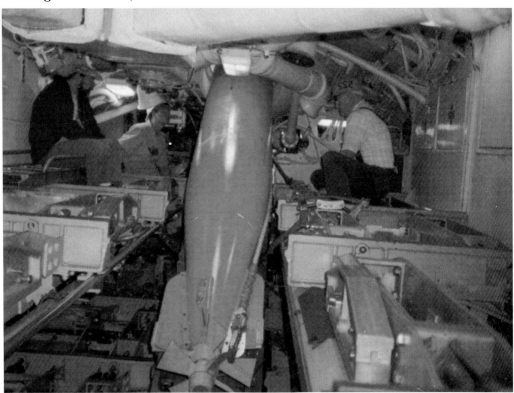

A Mark 14 torpedo is loaded gently into the forward torpedo room—not for action, but for display to the public. Photo courtesy of R. G. Walker.

Riding out the flood, the Blueback remained at dockside during the 1996 flooding of the Willamette River. The sub sustained no serious damage, but the access ramp and dock are under water. Photo courtesy of R. G. Walker.

CONTINUED FROM PAGE 16

He wanted to be in submarines ever since he first saw one, Hansen noted. "I had to put my tour in on a destroyer, but that was a good thing. I was a sonarman and that taught me from the surface down how anti-submarine warfare works. As a surface sonarman, they didn't test you on submarines, they tested you on surface craft. When my tour of duty expired I reenlisted to get on submarines." Hansen put in twenty-two years, and in that period received a commission, retiring as a Lieutenant Commander.

One man identified with the *Blueback* today is still a part of the submarine he served aboard. A technical advisor to the submarine museum, Lieutenant Commander L. Stuart (Stu) Taylor also served as the sub's engineering officer and for a time as the ship's Third Officer, in a tour of duty that lasted from 1965 through 1968. Like Hansen, he served in other vessels but the *Blueback* was special for him.

As a member of the submarine service Taylor knew hardships as well as rewards. An interviewer asked him the bad part of being a submariner. His reply: "Family separation. I never got to see my kids grow up. It was about the same as the surface Navy. For example, one year I was home four days. I have re-lived my kids growing up through my grandkids. Other than that, I could and would do it all again. The majority of sub duty is sea duty. Other than being on temporary additional duty to schools, most of the time for a subber is aboard the boat. In my whole career I probably put no more than four year's time ashore."

But, Taylor recalled, it seems he had little choice in selecting a career. "The reason I got into subs was that my dad was a Chief in the Navy, in World War I. He served, got out, and World War II broke out and he reenlisted. He ended up in charge of recruiting in our home town in 1945 and he had me pre-programmed from birth to go into the Navy. He recommended from the start to get in the subs; they pay better, feed better, and you're in port more often. That's true for the diesel boats, with the nukes it's another story."

His submarine service took him all over the world, including the coasts of Vietnam. "Our primary goal was to patrol the north end of the Tonkin Gulf in order to prevent any Russian or Chinese Communist subs from getting in there with the U.S. Seventh Fleet. When I was there we went in to rescue some pilots because the destroyers whose job that normally was, couldn't get in too close to shore. Basically the subs during both the Korean and Vietnam wars did the same thing subs did during World War II— except sink enemy ships.

"Today's submarine force goes to any place in the world where there's trouble. But most people don't know that."

Taylor remembers harrowing experiences in submarines, including an incident in the Barents Sea in which his submarine at the time, the USS *Tusk* (SS–426), was involved in a rescue of crew members from another submarine, the USS *Cochino* (SS–395), that had an explosion on board. In the middle of waves that towered thirty-five to forty feet, his sub managed to save the crewmen but lost seven of its own men. "There were a number of people on deck at the time, maybe fifteen, including me. As I left to go and had one foot through the hatch this tremendous wave came and wiped everything off the deck. Everybody and everything were cleared off. The wave threw me into the ship and to this day I don't know why I was lucky. Of the fourteen washed off, we were able to get seven back." In that incident, Taylor's sub took survivors, some of whom were badly injured, to Hammerfest in Norway, the nearest friendly port.

CONTINUED ON PAGE 54

25

What's out there? A young visitor peers through the Blueback's periscope during a visit to the submarine, one of thousands of visitors to the exhibit each year. Photo courtesy of R. G. Walker.

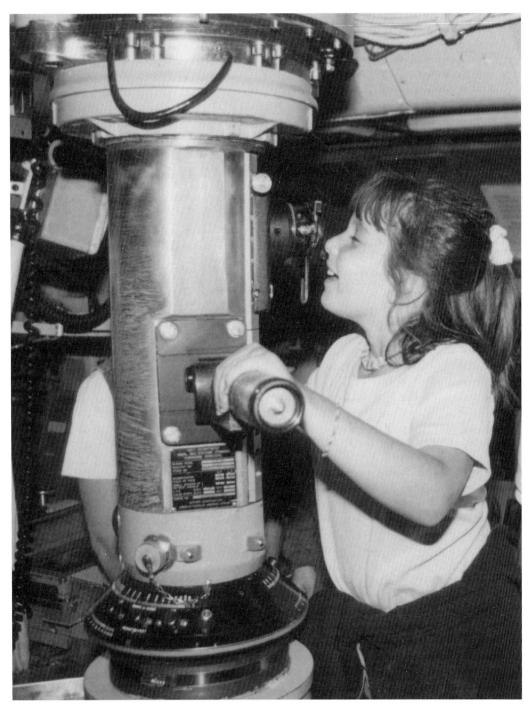

This young lady—a potential Navy Officer?—checks out the Blueback's periscope during a visiting program for youngsters managed by the Oregon Museum of Science and Industry. Tours are offered both daily and on weekends. Photo courtesy of R. G. Walker.

The submarine underway at sea. This photo shows the Blueback before the diving planes were installed on her sail (conning tower). U.S. Navy photo.

The Blueback broaches in a crescendo of white water. A broaching maneuver is used to get the submarine quickly to the surface, and involves blowing ballast to lighten the sub.

Driving the boat is a demanding task, requiring sailors to keep a sharp eye on instruments.

THE BLUEBACK IN STATISTICS

NAME: *Blueback* is the common name for the Sockeye, or Red Salmon, the most numerous of North American Pacific Salmon species.

BUILDER: Ingalls Shipbuilding Corporation, Pascagoula, Mississippi.

KEEL LAID: April 15,1957.

LAUNCHED: May 16,1959.

COMMISSIONED: October 15, 1959, Submarine Force, U.S. Pacific Fleet.

COST: $21 million.

FIRST DEPLOYED: March, 1961.

DECOMMISSIONED: October 1, 1990.

HULL DESIGN: Tear Drop (the first submarine to use this design).

DIMENSIONS: 219 feet long, 29-foot beam, 28-foot height.

DISPLACEMENT: On the surface, 2,158 tons; submerged, 2,649 tons.

COMPLEMENT: Eight officers, seventy-seven crew.

DESIGN DEPTH: 700 feet.

DESIGN SPEED: On the surface, 15 knots (17 mph); submerged snorkel, 12 knots (14 mph); submerged batteries, 21 knots (24 mph).

POWER: 3 Fairbanks-Morse 38d8 1/8 x 10 diesel engines
4800 brake horsepower (surface)
2 General Electric motors 3150 shaft horsepower (submerged)
1 shaft, 1 propeller.

FUEL CAPACITY: 112,000 gallons.

CRUISING DISTANCE: 19,000 miles without refueling.

WEAPONS: Torpedo Tubes six 21-inch tubes
Torpedoes 18 (six tube loaded).

SENSORS: Two periscopes, sonar, radar, Electronic Counter-Measures.

The Blueback rests easy alongside ASR 8, a submarine rescue vessel, in the calm waters of Pearl Harbor. U.S. Navy photo.

In a picture-postcard setting, the USS Blueback glides into the calm waters of Pearl Harbor, her home port. U.S. Navy photo.

Unaccustomed to being underway via someone else's power, the Blueback accepts a tow from a tug taking her in for drydock maintenance.

Photo courtesy of R. G. Walker.

36

On a break from her many patrols, the submarine lies at rest in the harbor at Hong Kong. U.S. Navy photo.

The submarine heads out to sea after a port visit in San Francisco.
U.S. Navy photo.

A Lieutenant carries out periscope operations. The 'scope becomes the eyes of the submarine when cruising at periscope depth.

On her way to take part in Portland's Rose Festival, the submarine pushes her way up the Columbia River. Photo courtesy of R. G. Walker.

A sister submarine of the Blueback, the USS Barbel, pushes her Tear-Drop shaped hull through the sea. U.S. Navy photo

44

Heading upstream toward Portland, the Blueback sails in front of a familiar landmark—the nuclear reactor at St. Helens, Oregon.
Photo courtesy of R. G. Walker.

At sea in the serene waters off Hawaii, the submarine cruises like any surface ship, but her true element is under the surface. U.S. Navy photo.

Primed in drydock, the submarine's garish paint is the undercoat for later coatings. The red paint protects against rust. Photo courtesy of R. G. Walker.

A stern view of the submarine in drydock shows the Blueback without her massive propeller. Photo courtesy of R. G. Walker.

Workers on deck of the Blueback sit on the sub's hull during the 1998 maintenance period in Cascade General Shipyard.
Photo courtesy of R. G. Walker.

Periodic repairs in drydock are necessary to keep the submarine at peak efficiency when she is at sea. Photo courtesy of R. G. Walker.

In her element, the Blueback cruises in the deep sea, threading her way among seamounts while moving silently toward her destination—perhaps a hostile coast, for reconnaissance.

The Submarine Verse of the Navy Hymn

Bless those who serve beneath the deep,

Through lonely hours their vigil keep.

May peace their mission ever be,

Protect each one we ask of thee.

Bless those at home who wait and pray,

For their return by night or day.

—Reverend Gale Williamson

Even at rest and during refurbishing, the Blueback projects an air of menace. Photo courtesy of R. G. Walker.

The propeller from the Blueback towers over a monument to all subs lost to the American Navy. The monument is on the river side of Portland's Oregon Museum of Science and Industry. Photo courtesy of R. G. Walker.

THE EVOLUTION OF SUBMARINES

1578—The first submarine design was drafted by William Borne, but was never more than a drawing. However, the principles were sound and still used today. Borne envisioned ballast tanks which could be filled to submerge and emptied to surface.

1620—Dutchman Cornelius Drebbel conceived and built a submarine powered by oars, and was the first to address the problem of how to replenish the air inside.

1776—David Bushnell built a one-man submarine called the *Turtle*. The Colonial Army tried to sink the British HMS *Eagle* with it, but failed. Bushnell's invention was the first sub to dive, surface, and be used in combat.

1798—Robert Fulton built a submarine using a sail while on the surface and a hand-cranked screw while submerged. He called it the *Nautilus*.

1895—John Holland introduced the Holland VII and the following year the Holland VIII. The submarines had a petroleum engine for running on the surface and an electric engine for submerged operations. His design was used by all the world's navies and was current to 1914.

1904—The French built the submarine *Aigrette* which was the first sub to use diesel fuel for propulsion on the surface and an electric engine for submerged operations. The diesel engine used fuel less volatile than petroleum, and diesel fuel became the preferred fuel for submarines.

1943—The German U-boat, U-264, was equipped with a snorkel; it provided air to the diesel engine and allowed the sub to operate at a shallow depth to recharge the batteries.

1944—Another German boat, the U-791, used hydrogen peroxide as an alternative fuel source.

1954—America launched the first nuclear-powered submarine, the USS *Nautilus*, the first true submersible, able to operate underwater indefinitely. The sub's development was brought about by a team of Navy, government, and contracted engineers. The team was headed by Captain Hyman G. Rickover.

1958—The Navy introduced the USS *Albacore*, which has a Tear Drop design hull to reduce underwater resistance and make for greater speed and maneuverability.

1959—The USS *George Washington* conducted the first successful launch of a Polaris missile and ushered in the era of the Fleet Ballistic Missile Submarines. The sub was the first of forty-one such vessels, which prowled the world's seas during the 1960s and 1970s.

1967—The Sturgeon class subs made their debut.

1976—The Los Angeles class of nuclear subs came into being.

1981—The Ohio class of submarines are the largest subs ever built by the United States, with a hull 560 feet long. The submarines were constructed to carry Trident missiles.

1991—The USS *Louisville* became the first submarine to launch a cruise missile (a Tomahawk) against an enemy target. The action came during Operation Desert Storm, the war in the Persian Gulf.

1997—The Seawolf class of nuclear subs appeared in the Navy arsenal.

CURRENTLY—To be built in the years 2004–2007 are submarines to be designated the Virginia class of SSN subs, to be 377 feet long and built to carry Tomahawk missiles. A scaled replica of the Virginia class, the LSV (large-scale vehicle) *Cutthroat*, was in the planning stages as the millennium closed. The 200-ton unmanned stealth test vessel was envisioned as relatively inexpensive craft for testing future submarines, and the test of the LSV itself was planned to take place in Lake Pend Oreille in northern Idaho.

CONTINUED FROM PAGE 25

Off Pearl Harbor, while running at test depth of about 700 feet, the *Blueback* was almost lost because of a relatively small malfunction. "I was up in the wardroom when someone called and said Mr. Taylor can you get back to maneuvering immediately" Taylor recalled. "I shot through the sub. When I got back to the maneuvering room I looked about and there was an air-equip hose that's ordinarily about an inch, inch and a half, and now about six inches. I grabbed the mike and yelled 'get us up to periscope depth immediately—possible flooding.' As we went up the hose shrank, returning to normal size. But if that thing had blown at 700 feet I figured it would have killed our propulsion and we'd be at the bottom of the Pacific right now. That's how close it was."

Another incident took place off the coast of North Korea as the *Blueback* was moving shoreward to land an agent. Taylor had the con (control of the sub), and remembered the incident this way:

"We were coming in late at night, traveling at about 200 feet below the surface . . . I was coming up to get radio messages, but before surfacing you had to listen hard, to make sure there was nothing near us. First thing you do is raise the periscope, make a rapid 360-degree sweep to make sure nothing is near. I heard nothing and we started up. At about one hundred feet I started raising the periscope (it would extend about 60 feet). Just as I was raising it I heard this awful grating sound like chains dragging in gravel. Quickly I said 'down two hundred feet.' So we went back down . . . I listened again.

"Finally we surfaced again. When we got up far enough I put the periscope up again and did the 360. What I saw was this—a whole bunch of those wooden-hulled junks, crews sleeping all night, no lights anywhere. So we surmised that what I had done was take the periscope and rammed it through the bottom of one of those hulls. Over to one side on the surface I could see lights going, guys running around, yelling. We descended to 200 feet and took off.

"The next morning at light we surfaced. I climbed up on the bridge because I wanted to see what had happened to the periscope and they raised the periscope, and just the paint was scratched.

"So they gave me credit for sinking the most peacetime tonnage that year."

Not everyone could be a submariner. Qualifications had to be met, as Taylor remembered: "The initial quals are more rigorous than those you have to pass when you qualify for a new assignment/boat. You pick up the differences. There are three levels of qualifications: (1) The enlisted quals, which usually takes about nine months, (basically you have to show proficiency that you knew every system, every valve on board); (2) Then there's the officer's quals, which took a minimum of a year, normally. In addition to all that the enlisted were expected to know, the officer had to hold each of the officer's positions aboard the boat until you could perform any of them—plus you had to know all the signal lights, and you had to have been able to make so many torpedo hits, and you had to do it underways, and landings; and (3) The qualifications for command—you wrote a thesis and it had to be approved by a Commodore and Division Commander and then your Commanding Officer."

Even once qualified for command, Taylor said, you had to keep learning. "As an officer you had to qualify first on your own submarine and then you went to a different class of sub and qualified in port, dealing with emergencies and so forth. Then you had to go to yet another class of submarine and get it underway and do all the things at sea."

For those who did qualify and become a part of the Silent Service, the rewards were long and lasting, not the least of which are the memories of an adventurous life and a satisfying profession. Most men would agree with the Navy slogan: it's not a job, it's an adventure.

Submariners are fond of saying there are two kinds of ships: submarines and targets.

Such bravado is a part of the submarine service that has known a tradition of pride and accomplishments that go back a century, and has never diminished. Submariners think of themselves as a special breed and their record since 1900 bears it out.

It was October 12, 1900, that the U.S. Submarine Force came into being with the commissioning of the Navy's first sub, the USS *Holland*. For the first few years of their existence submarines were used with coastal and harbor defense. By 1906 the Navy decided that submarines were the best defense America had against an attack on the West Coast, since most of the Navy's ships were in the Atlantic Fleet. The subs were assigned the defense role until the battle fleet could arrive from the Atlantic. The Secretary of the Navy also took the position that submarines were vital to the defense of the important U.S. naval base of Subic Bay, in the Philippines, so subs were positioned there.

The early years were a time of intense research and development in the construction of subs and of their roles in wartime. There were advances in propulsion systems and the periscope, and improvements in the double hull design of subs. The interval before World War II was a period of technological advances and of tactical training. The time was well spent, for in the shattering of peace on December 7, 1941, the submarines came into their own.

The Japanese attack on the U.S. Pacific Fleet at Pearl Harbor was a tactical blunder. The raid failed to destroy the fuel storage tanks, failed to take out the Pearl Harbor Naval Shipyard, and failed to destroy the submarine pens. Even the focus on the capital ships turned out to be a mistake, for of the eight battleships sunk that day, six were refloated, repaired, and put into action. Three damaged cruisers were repaired and saw action. Among the first ships to carry the war to the enemy were the submarines, holding the line in the Pacific and permitting a strategy of defeating Hitler in Europe before dealing with the Japanese. The subs' bold actions also gave the shipyards time to repair the vessels damaged in the Pearl Harbor attack.

Only three days after the Pearl Harbor attack, the USS *Triton* carried out an attack on Japanese shipping south of Wake Island. By the end of the first year of war with Japan, U.S. subs had accomplished three hundred and fifty war patrols. The variety of their missions is impressive: they provided coastal defense in the Lingayen Gulf, Java, and Midway; carried out a blockade in the Truk-Solomon Islands area; intercepted Japanese capital ships and merchant shipping; took part in commando raids in Makin; delivered and retrieved guerrillas and spies for reconnaissance in the Marshall Islands; helped evacuate people from Corregidor.

Submarines also served as mobile weather stations and as beacons for air strikes from carriers, such as Jimmy Doolittle's initial raid over Tokyo. By the end of 1942, submarines had sunk one hundred and eighty Japanese merchant ships totaling 725,000 tons.

The next year saw an increase in submarine activity. During three hundred and fifty war patrols the subs fired four thousand torpedoes and sank three hundred and thirty-five enemy ships. Young skippers and crew conducted aggressive patrols, particularly in the East China Sea and around Japan itself. In 1943 some 1.5 million tons of Japanese shipping fell victim to the prowling U.S. subs. The Japanese Merchant Marine began to fall behind, unable to keep pace with the losses that included twenty percent of its non-tanker capability.

Because of aggressive patrolling, U.S. sub losses also increased—fifteen boats were lost in action.

The next year, 1944, was a time of terror for Japanese shipping, as American submarines roamed like wolf packs across the Pacific. Almost sixty-one hundred torpedoes were fired during five hundred and twenty war patrols; six hundred and three ships totaling 2.7 million tons went to the bottom as a result of U.S. submarines pressing home their attacks. The subs' constant menace and the success of their attacks shut down Japan's flow of oil from the south up to the homeland, severely inhibiting the Japanese ability to carry on the war. For Japan it was a long and bloody year in which U.S. subs sank seven aircraft carriers, a battleship, nine cruisers, and about thirty destroyers. Sadly, nineteen U.S. subs and their crews were lost.

The year 1944 was also a time when subs were into the rescue business in a big way. With the stepped-up bombing of Japanese targets, subs were stationed at strategic points from Tokyo Bay to the South Pacific to pick up downed U.S. airmen. Eighty-six subs were assigned to such duty at one time or another, and rescued five hundred and four pilots, including a future U.S. President, George Bush.

After the war, when the histories were written and summaries recorded, the record of the submariners was astonishing: a force of fifty thousand men, including back-up and staff personnel—less than two percent of the U.S. Navy—accounted for a staggering fifty-five percent of Japan's maritime losses. From 1941 through 1945, U.S. subs sank eleven hundred and thirteen vessels, and caused a disruption in Japan's oil and commerce flow, one of the primary reasons for her defeat. Japan's merchant fleet was composed of six million tons at the start of the war; U.S. subs sank close to five million tons.

The price was necessary, but heavy. Of two hundred and eighty-eight submarines in action, fifty-two were lost, with the deaths of some thirty-five hundred men. Seven submariners received the Medal of Honor during World War II, two posthumously.

The end of that war was not the end of activity for U.S. subs, for other wars were soon to test the submariners' skills. With the outbreak of the Korean conflict in 1950, submarines once again were among the first on the scene. Fleet boats screened naval surface forces that provided tactical air support, surveyed Soviet and Korean mine fields, and took part in special forces raids. Potential amphibious landing sites were photographed by U.S. subs in support of the daring landing at Inchon. Few Soviet ships sailed the Pacific without being watched by American subs, and their presence in the Formosa Straits and the Sea of Okhotsk was a powerful deterrent.

The Cold War brought new challenges. In Admiral Sergei Gorshkov, the Soviets had a naval leader who was a strong proponent of submarine warfare, and subs became the focal point of an aggressive naval expansion policy. The Soviets built technologically-advanced submarines that were quieter, faster, and could go deeper. America countered with subs that matched or exceeded the Soviet versions, and the Soviets financial and industrial resources could not keep pace with America's commitment to more powerful subs.

In January 1955, the USS *Nautilus* sent its famous message: "underway on nuclear power." Since then, nuclear-powered subs have been the principal weapon against surface ships and other submarines. On July 20, 1960, the USS *George Washington* conducted the first successful launch of a Polaris ballistic missile. Since those milestones, the cruise missile-equipped nuclear-powered submarines have been a first line of defense—as they have always been. The USS *Blueback* was the last non-nuclear submarine built by the Navy, and the last to be decommissioned, after thirty-one years of faithful service.

The shadowy war in Vietnam's jungles and highlands was occasion for continued submarine actions. Subs conducted patrols that included intelligence-gathering and other missions still classified.

During its one hundred years the "Silent Service" has proven to be a significant asset to America's sea power and has become a primary deterrent to enemy ambitions. The Service has done more, participating in scientific expeditions to add to the world's body of knowledge, taken part in ecological studies of marine life, participated in

SUBMARINER'S LANGUAGE

The Navy has its own language, based on traditions or sometimes, it seems, on whimsy.

Submariners, too, speak a language that is sometimes a kind of shorthand and sometimes simply jargon, but given legitimacy by time and usage. Here is a short sampling of the submarine service's colorful vocabulary:

BOOMERS—The nickname for Strategic Missile Submarines.

GOAT LOCKER—The term for the Chief Petty Officers' quarters on a sub.

ANGLES AND DANGLES—The test conducted by a submarine to make sure everything is stowed properly before starting a mission; it calls for making up-and-down movements of the sub, plus using large rudder angles at moderate speeds.

PLANK OWNERS—The original crew of a boat at the time it is commissioned.

SNAPSHOT—The procedure for launching a torpedo in an emergency.

SAIL—Not something made of canvas to catch the wind; a sub's sail is the narrow tower (superstructure) on a sub, containing the main sensors, periscopes, radar, radio antennas, a small bridge for lookouts, etc.

HEAD—The washroom, or toilet.

U-BOAT—Unterseeboot. The German word for submarine.

salvage and rescue operations, and gathered data about the world's oceans that have added significantly to the understanding of the ecology and geography of the oceans.

Submariners can look back to a century of achievements—and forward to continued important contributions to America's defense, and the world's safety.

The Architecture of the Blueback (SS 581)

1. Officer's Staterooms
2. Wardroom
3. Radio Room
4. Crypto Room
5. Control Room and
   Attack Center
6. Sonar Room
7. Crew's Washroom
8. Torpedo Room
9. 6 Torpedo Tube
10. Store Room
11. 2 Propulsion Batteries
12. Galley and Crew's Mess
13. 3 Diesel Engines
14. 3 Electric Generators
15. Manuevering Room
16. 2 Propulsion Electric Motors

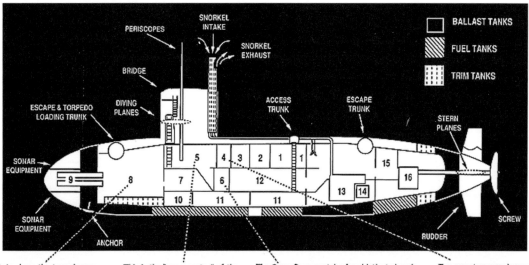

This is where the torpedoes or mines were stored; torpedo tubes were always loaded. (When space was tight, some crewmen actually slept among the torpedoes!)

This is the "nerve center" of the Blueback, where navigation, steering, diving and surfacing, speed control and torpedo firing equipment are located.

The Sonar Room contained sophisticated equipment used to interpret sound vibrations picked up by the sub's electronic "ears." Sonar operators identified the sounds as ships, other subs, whales, etc by their specific sonar signatures.

Top-secret commands were received and decoded here; an exterior-locking door kept the radio operators secured inside during critical operations.

Courtesy Oregon Museum of Science and Industry

The Blueback arriving in San Diego. The submarine once ran from Yokosuka, Japan, to San Diego, 5340 miles, underwater. U.S. Navy photo.

The level of the Willamette River rises and falls, gently moving the hull of the great submarine in a familiar rhythm. It is a hull that has known far distant seas and more than one ocean. For thirty-one years the Blueback served her country on active duty, winning honor after honor on missions that contributed significantly to keeping America free and keeping the sea lanes safe during a difficult and dangerous time. She did all that was asked of her, and more.

She had her admirers then, and admirers now. Those who served aboard remember a proud and powerful warship, a credit to the nation that gave her birth, as were the submariners themselves. They were elite sailors, on an elite ship. Today the Blueback is positioned where visitors can board and browse, getting a feel for the technology of a great vessel, and perhaps feeling the presence of those men who served aboard. Perhaps the visitors hear soft footsteps and the dim echo of their voices, and picture the crew as the sailors went about their duties.

The Blueback has received her own honorable discharge from active duty. On May 15, 1994, the submarine was opened to the public, as a means of introducing visitors to the fascinating world of undersea exploration—and as a reminder of the dedication and patriotism of the men who go down to the sea, and under it.

ACKNOWLEDGMENTS AND CREDITS

The creators of this book are grateful to the various people and Navy commands who assisted with this book; none is to be held liable for any errors, for which the author assumes responsibility.

Helpful were R. G. Walker, Submarine Manager for the Oregon Museum of Science and Industry; Gary Bock, OMSI, the *Blueback*'s Submarine Overnights Coordinator; L. Stuart Taylor (Lieutenant Commander, USN-Ret); Richard N. Hansen (Lieutenant Commander, USN-Ret); and James R. (Pat) Patterson, (Chief Electronics Technician, USN-Ret). All of these gentlemen in the Portland, Oregon, area gave freely of their time and advice.

Also helpful were LCDR Jim Doody, Military Editor, Undersea Warfare Magazine; Rick Dau, Director, Operations and Public Affairs, National Submarine League; and Al Schor, who served on the USS *Tusk* (SS-426) from 1956 to 1959.

In the Pacific we are indebted to Senior Chief Journalist (SW/AW) Darrell Ames, USN, of the staff of Commander, Submarine Force Pacific, at Pearl Harbor, Hawaii, and to Erik Stone on Guam.

THE WRITER

Commander Scott C. S. Stone (USNR-Ret) is a national prize-winning novelist, a biographer, historian, and veteran foreign correspondent. Pursuing dual careers, his military service includes ground combat in two wars, duty aboard a destroyer and a cruiser, and service with paramilitary units sailing Chinese junks in wartime. He has had twenty-three books published prior to this one.

THE ILLUSTRATOR

Arthur (Gene) Ellis is as well known for his versatility as for the quality of his work. He is illustrator, animator, cinematographer, sculptor, still photographer, and has worked as art director on several feature films. He has traveled extensively, including a photo journey to the South Pole. Ellis is a veteran of the Navy's famed Pacific Combat Camera Group.

THE RESEARCHER

Bill Aull has spent much of his time in creative capacities, primarily as a college-level teacher of writing. Also a Navy veteran, Aull is accustomed to wearing several hats, as public relations specialist, technical editor of a literary quarterly, and as a teacher at Clark College in Vancouver, Washington.